The Wonder of Christmas
Once You Believe, Anything Is Possible
Children's Leader Guide

The Wonder of Christmas
Once You Believe, Anything Is Possible

The Wonder of Christmas
978-1-5018-2322-0 *Book*
978-1-5018-2323-7 *eBook*
978-1-5018-2324-4 *Large Print*

The Wonder of Christmas: Leader Guide
978-1-5018-2325-1 *Book*
978-1-5018-2326-8 *eBook*

The Wonder of Christmas: DVD
978-1-5018-2329-9

**The Wonder of Christmas:
Devotions for the Season**
978-1-5018-2327-5 *Book*
978-1-5018-2328-2 *eBook*

**The Wonder of Christmas:
Children's Leader Guide**
978-1-5018-2336-7

**The Wonder of Christmas:
Youth Study Book**
978-1-5018-2334-3 *Book*
978-1-5018-2335-0 *eBook*

The Wonder of Christmas: Worship Planning
978-1-5018-2337-4 *Flash Drive*
978-1-5018-2338-1 *Download*

Ed Robb & Rob Renfroe

THE *Wonder* OF CHRISTMAS

ONCE YOU BELIEVE, ANYTHING IS POSSIBLE

Children's Leader Guide
by Sally Hoelscher

Abingdon Press / Nashville

The Wonder of Christmas
Once You Believe, Anything Is Possible

Children's Leader Guide
by Sally Hoelscher

Copyright © 2016 Abingdon Press
All rights reserved.

ISBN 978-1-5018-2336-7

16 17 18 19 20 21 22 23 24 25 — 10 9 8 7 6 5 4 3 2 1

Contents

To the Leader

This children's leader guide is designed for use with the churchwide Advent program *The Wonder of Christmas: Once You Believe, Anything is Possible* by Ed Robb and Rob Renfroe. This guide includes four lessons—one for each Sunday in Advent—that help children explore the wonder of the Christmas story. (*Note*: This study begins with the story of the wise men following the star and ends with Isaiah's prophecy. Although not chronological, the order of the lessons was chosen to correspond with the weekly themes of the other program components so that all ages are studying the same material each week. If you prefer to tell the story to your children in chronological order, feel free to switch the order of lessons 1 and 4.)

Lesson Plan Format

The lessons in this guide, designed for children in grades K–2 and 3–6, are presented in a large group/small group format. Children begin with time spent at activity centers, followed by time together as a large group. Children end the lesson in small groups determined by age. Each lesson plan contains the following sections:

Focus for the Teacher

The information in this section will provide you with background information about the week's lesson. Use this section for your own study as you prepare.

Explore Interest Groups

You'll find in this section ideas for a variety of activity centers. The activities will prepare the children to hear the Bible story. Allow the children to choose one or more of the activities that interest them. Occasionally there will be an activity that is recommended for all children, usually because it relates directly to a later activity. When this is the case, it will be noted in the sidebar notes.

Large Group

The children will come together as a large group to hear the story for the week. This section begins with a transition activity followed by the story and a Bible verse activity. A worship time concludes the large group time.

Small Groups

Children are divided into age-level groups for small-group time. Depending on the size of your class, you may need to have more than one group for each age level. It is recommended that each small group contain no more than ten children.

Younger Children
The activities in this section are designed for children in grades K–2.

Older Children
The activities in this section are designed for children in grades 3–6.

Reproducible Pages

At the end of each lesson are reproducible pages, to be photocopied and handed out for all the children to use during that lesson's activities.

Schedule

Many churches have weeknight programs that include an evening meal, an intergenerational gathering time, and classes for children, youth, and adults. The following schedule illustrates one way to organize a weeknight program.

5:30 p.m.	Meal
6:00 p.m.	Intergenerational gathering introducing weekly themes and places for the lesson. This time may include presentations, skits, music, and opening or closing prayers.
6:15 p.m.–8:15 p.m.	Classes for children, youth, and adults.

Churches may want to do this study as a Sunday school program. This setting would be similar to the weeknight setting. The following schedule takes into account a shorter class time, which is the norm for Sunday morning programs.

10 minutes	Intergenerational gathering
45 minutes	Classes for children, youth, and adults

Choose a schedule that works best for your congregation and its existing Christian education programs.

Blessings to you and the children as you explore the wonder of Christmas.

1 The Wonder of a Star

Objectives

The children will:
- hear Matthew 2:1-12.
- learn about the magi following a star to search for a new king.
- discover that the magi paid attention to the sign of the star.
- explore what it means for them to pay attention to messages from God.

Theme

The Christmas story points us to God.

Bible Verse

Give thanks to the only one who makes great wonders—God's faithful love lasts forever.

(Psalm 136:4)

Focus for the Teacher

"My whole being thirsts for God, for the living God. / When will I come and see God's face?" (Psalm 42:2). In this verse, the psalmist puts into words a feeling that many throughout history have experienced. We wonder about God. There is a part of us that searches for God, that longs to know God is with us.

The wise men took action to fulfill this longing. These magi came from a land in the east. They may have been astrologers. They saw a new star in the sky. They could have said, "Oh, look, a new star—that's interesting," and gone on with their lives. Instead they let themselves wonder about the star. "What does it mean? Has a new king been born?" The magi interpreted the appearance of the star to mean a new leader was about to be born. Something compelled them to follow the star. They began a journey—a journey that would lead them to Jesus.

The magi were Gentiles, non-Jewish people. The magi, or wise men, had not been waiting for the birth of the Messiah for hundreds of years as the Jews had. It was the star—the wonder of the star—that led the magi to Jesus. Even though

> It was the star that led the magi to Jesus.

the magi had not been anticipating the birth of the Messiah as the Jews had, when they reached Bethlehem, they were filled with joy.

When the wise men made their journey, they didn't come empty-handed. They brought gifts. These weren't just any gifts. The wise men brought gold, frankincense, and myrrh—gifts that were worthy of a king. When they found Jesus, they knelt down and worshiped him, honoring him with their treasures.

We don't usually begin the Advent season talking about the wise men. We usually tell the story of the magi on Epiphany, January 6, the last day of the Christmas season. Encountering the magi early in the Advent season is unexpected—just as the appearance of a new star was unexpected for those magi. At the appearance of the star, the magi set out on a journey to discover the new king. Like the magi, we are also on a journey—a journey of preparation to celebrate the birth of that same king. The wondrous star that led the wise men to Bethlehem invites us to search for God this Advent season.

Explore Interest Groups

Be sure that adult leaders are waiting when the first child arrives. Greet and welcome the children. Get the children involved in an activity that interests them and introduces the theme for the day's activities.

Discover Today's Wonder Word

- **Say:** We are beginning a four-week study called *The Wonder of Christmas*. Each week we will have a different wonder word to explore.

- Show the children the poster you have prepared.

- **Say:** Today's wonder word is hidden on this poster.

- Invite the children to work together and use blue and purple markers to color over the entire poster. Because the marker will not cover the areas where the white crayon has been used, the hidden word will become visible. Show the children how to use the flat edge of the marker tip to color.

- **Ask:** What is today's wonder word? (star)

- **Say:** Today we will be discussing the wonder of a star!

- **Ask:** Do you remember hearing about a star in the Christmas story? (the star that led the wise men or magi to Bethlehem)

- Display the finished poster in your classroom. Leave the poster on display throughout the study.

Prepare

- ✓ *Note*: Consider having all children participate in this activity since it provides the theme for today's lesson.

- ✓ Provide a large piece of posterboard, white crayon, blue and purple markers, and tape.

- ✓ Use a white crayon to write the word *star* in large bubble letters on the posterboard.

- ✓ *Tip*: If the posterboard you are using has a shiny side, use the non-shiny surface of the posterboard for this activity.

- ✓ *Note*: If you have a large class, prepare multiple posters and divide the children into small groups for this activity.

Prepare

✓ Provide construction paper (yellow, gold, or white for traditional star colors or red and green for Christmas colors), staplers, and ribbon or yarn.

✓ Cut construction paper strips 3/4-inches by 6-inches. Use a paper cutter to quickly cut the strips.

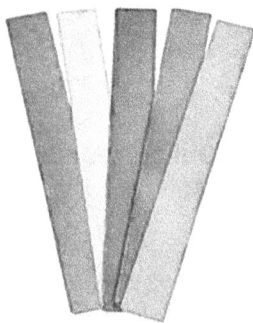

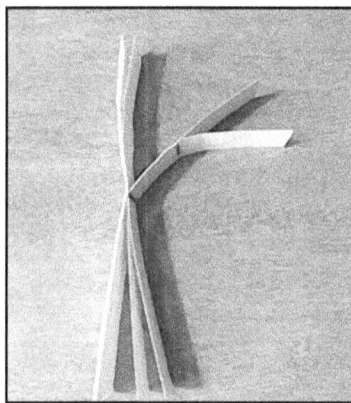

Make a Star Ornament

• Invite each child to choose five strips of construction paper.

• Have each child stack their strips of paper on top of each other horizontally.

• Instruct each child to fold the strips in half from end to end (from left to right), crease the fold to mark the center of the strips, and then unfold the strips.

• Let each child staple all five strips of paper together in the fold or crease mark.

• Have each child staple two of the adjacent strips together about 1 inch from the center.

• Let each child continue to staple the remaining adjacent pairs of strips together about 1 inch from the center, until there are five pairs of stapled strips—creating five distinct arms.

• Have each child separate the ends of one arm, putting a finger between the two strips, and then repeat this step with an adjacent arm. Instruct the child to look at these four strips and staple together the two inside strips at the end or tip—stapling a strip of one arm to a strip of the other arm. (This should form a diamond shape when the end is pressed toward the center.)

• Encourage each child to continue separating and stapling the remaining arms in this manner together at the ends (four more times).

• Invite each child to gently use their fingers to shape the ornament into a star by creasing the paper slightly near the middle (center) staple points.

• Have each child cut a piece of ribbon or yarn about 12 inches long, thread it through the ornament and tie the ends together to form a hanging loop.

• **Say:** When you take your ornament home, hang it on your tree to remind you of the wonder of a star.

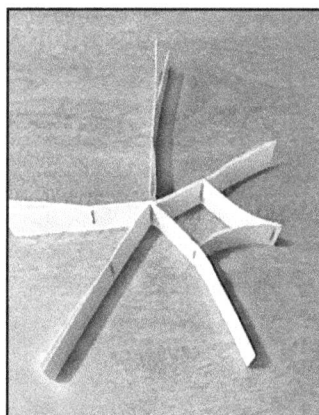

Ribbon Shapes

- Have each child cut a piece of ribbon 3 feet long.
- If you have a large class, divide the children into groups of ten.
- Have the children stand in a circle.
- **Say:** Place your ribbon in your right hand and hold it by one end. Reach your left hand out and pick up the end of your neighbor's ribbon.
- Have the children step back until the ribbons are tight, but not so far back they are hard to hold onto.
- **Say:** Right now you are forming in a circle. Today we are talking about the wonder of a star.
- Challenge the children to form themselves into a star.
- Allow the children to work together to form the star, offering assistance only if necessary.
- Once children have figured out how to form a star, have them practice to see how quickly they can transition from a circle to a star.
- Have the children experiment making other shapes, such as a square or a triangle.
- Challenge the children to transition from each shape back into their star.
- **Alternate activity:** If you have fewer than ten children in your class, cut ten 3-foot lengths of ribbon and have the children work together to lay the ribbon on the floor in the shape of a star.

Prepare

✓ Provide ribbon, scissors, and yardsticks or rulers.

Prepare

✓ Make copies of **Reproducible 1b: Triangle Stars** on cardstock.

✓ Provide large sheets of construction paper (12 x 18), scissors, and glue sticks.

Triangle Stars

- Give each child a copy of **Triangle Stars** and a pair of scissors.

- Have each child cut out twelve triangles by cutting on the solid lines.

- **Say:** All of the shapes you cut out are triangles, but it is possible to put them together to form a star shape. Depending on which corners of the triangles you put together in the center, you will make one of three possible star patterns.

- Encourage each child to experiment with arranging his or her triangles to form all three possible star patterns.

- **Say:** Note that if you put the smallest corners of the triangles in the center, you will form a twelve-pointed star.

- **Ask:** What happens if you put the medium corners of the triangles in the center? (You will form a six-pointed star using only six triangles.) What happens if you put the largest corners of the triangles in the center? (You will form a four-pointed star using only four triangles.)

- Have each child choose a large piece of construction paper.

- Invite each child to glue triangles on the construction paper to form either one twelve-pointed star, two six-pointed stars, or three four-pointed stars.

- **Say:** There is a star in today's Bible story.

- **Ask:** Do you know any Bible stories about stars?

Large Group

Bring all the children together to experience the Bible story. Use a bell to alert the children to the large group time.

Learn Some Signs

- **Say:** For the next four weeks we are going to be talking about wonder. Right now we are going to learn to say the word *wonder* using sign language.
- Teach the children the sign for wonder: Place your right index finger to your temple as if you are pointing to the side of your head and move your finger in a small circle.
- Invite the children to make the sign for wonder with you.
- **Say:** Today we are talking about the wonder of a star.
- Teach the children the sign for star: Hold both index fingers close to each other and above your head as if you are pointing to the sky. Alternating fingers, move one up as you move the other down. Do this several times. This represents the stars twinkling.
- Invite the children to make the sign for star with you.
- **Say:** Now, let's sign the words *wonder* and *star* together.
- Encourage the children to sign the word *wonder* and then sign the word *star*.

Prepare

✓ Review the instructions for making the signs for *wonder* and *promise* so you can teach them to the children.

Magi Follow a Star

- **Say:** Today is the first Sunday of Advent. Advent is a time of waiting and preparation.
- **Ask:** What are we waiting and preparing for during Advent? (Christmas)
- **Say:** During Advent we prepare to once again celebrate the birth of Jesus. One of the things we do during Advent is retell the stories of Jesus' birth. So far today we have talked a lot about stars.
- **Ask:** Do you know a Christmas story that involves a star? (the story of the wise men)
- **Say:** You are right! The wise men followed a star. We don't usually begin Advent with the story of the wise men. Often the story of the wise men is one of the last Christmas stories we hear. After all, the wise men traveled from far away, so it took them a long time to reach Bethlehem. They were not Jesus' first visitors. So it's a little unexpected to begin with the story of the wise men, but that's okay. Unexpected things make us pay attention and wonder. Let's hear the story.
- Invite your volunteers to read the story from **Magi Follow a Star**.
- Thank your readers for telling today's story.
- **Ask:** Why did the wise men go to Bethlehem? (They followed the star. To search for a new king.)

Prepare

✓ Provide copies of **Reproducible 1a: Magi Follow a Star** for children to take home.

✓ Recruit three confident readers to share the story. Give each child a copy of **Magi Follow a Star** and assign parts.

✓ *Option:* Recruit three volunteers to come to your class and tell the story. Give them copies of **Magi Follow a Star**.

Prepare

✓ Write the Bible verse on a large piece of mural paper and hang it where the children can see it. (Give thanks to the only one who makes great wonders—God's faithful love lasts forever. Psalm 136:4) Leave the Bible verse on display throughout the entire study.

Prepare

✓ Provide a Nativity set and an Advent wreath with LED candles that will be used throughout the study.

✓ Set up a worship center by covering a table with a cloth. Add a Bible and the Advent wreath. Place the wise men figures from the Nativity set on one side of the table. If your Nativity set contains a stable, set the stable on the other side of the table. Do not add the other pieces of the Nativity set to the worship center.

Learn the Bible Verse

- **Say:** Our Bible verse for the next four weeks is from the Book of Psalms.
- Show the children the Bible verse.
- Encourage the children to read the verse with you.
- **Say:** This verse reminds us that the God who created our wonderful world loves us—and will always love us.
- Divide the children into two groups.
- **Say:** Now we are going to divide our verse into two parts. The first part will be, "Give thanks to the only one who makes great wonders." The second part will be, "God's faithful love lasts forever." When I point to your group, you will say the first part of the Bible verse. The other group will then complete the verse by saying the second part.
- Point to each group several times and encourage the children to say the Bible verse.

The Wonder of a Star

- **Say:** One thing we sometimes do to help us wait and prepare during Advent is to light candles on an Advent wreath.
- Invite a child to turn on one of the LED candles on the Advent wreath.
- **Say:** Because today is the first Sunday of Advent, we light one candle.
- **Ask:** How many Sundays are there in Advent? (four)
- **Say:** Our worship center has a Bible on it to remind us that the stories we hear during Advent are from the Bible.
- **Ask:** What else do you see on our worship center? (wise men)
- **Say:** Today we heard the story of the wise men. I've placed them on the edge of the worship center to show they are beginning their journey. We haven't heard the story of Jesus' birth yet. It took the wise men time to reach Bethlehem and find Jesus. They are still searching.
- **Ask:** What if the wise men hadn't paid attention to the new star that appeared? How would the story be different if the magi had ignored the star?
- Allow children an opportunity to share their ideas.
- **Say:** The wise men were paying attention and they noticed a new star in the sky. But the wise men did more than pay attention. They also acted. They interpreted the appearance of the new star as a message that a new king had been born. And then they went in search of the new king. The story of the wise men and the wonder of a star reminds us to pay attention during Advent.
- **Pray:** God, whose love for us is never-ending, thank you for the story of Christmas. As we retell the smaller stories within the big story of the birth of your Son, Jesus, help us to pay attention. Amen.
- Dismiss children to their small groups.

Small Groups

Divide the children into small groups. You may organize the groups around age levels or around readers and nonreaders. Keep the groups small, with a maximum of ten children in each group. You may need to have more than one group of each age level.

Young Children

- **Say:** Today you are going to begin making an art journal. You will add to your art journal every week during Advent. First you will make a cover for your art journal.
- Invite each child to choose a piece of large construction paper.
- Have each child fold the construction paper in half by bringing the short sides together.
- Give each child a copy of **Journal Cover**.
- Encourage each child to use crayons or markers to decorate the journal cover and add their name.
- Have each child cut out the cover and glue it onto the front of the construction paper folder.
- **Say:** Now you are ready to make the first page for your art journal.
- **Ask:** What is our wonder word today? (star) What does a star have to do with our Bible story? (the wise men followed a star) Why did the wise men follow the star? (to find a new king, to find Jesus)
- **Say:** When the star first appeared, the wise men wondered what it meant. The star ended up leading the wise men to God's Son.
- **Ask:** Who is God's Son? (Jesus)
- **Say:** The star led the way for the wise men to find Jesus. Just as the star directed the wise men to God's son, the stories of Christmas point us to God. As we retell the stories of Jesus' birth each year, we learn more about God.
- Give each child a copy of **The Wonder of a Star** and have the child write his or her name on it.
- **Say:** On this first page of your art journal, design and decorate a star that points people to God.
- Invite each child to use crayons or markers to decorate the star.
- Encourage children to tell you about their stars.
- Have children place their stars inside their art journal covers.
- Collect the art journals to be used next week.
- Have the children sit in a circle.
- Invite the children to make the signs for wonder and star learned earlier in the lesson.
- **Pray:** God of wonder, thank you for the star that led the wise men to your Son, Jesus. Amen.

Prepare

- ✓ Provide large sheets of construction paper (12 x 18), crayons, markers, scissors, and paper clips.
- ✓ Make copies of **Reproducible 1c: Journal Cover** and **Reproducible 1d: The Wonder of a Star** for each child.
- ✓ *Tip:* Make extra art journal covers to have for children who are not here this week.
- ✓ *Tip:* Provide paper clips so that the children may secure their pages inside their journals until the last week when they staple their books together.

Prepare

✓ Provide large sheets of construction paper, colored pencils, crayons, markers, scissors, and paper clips.

✓ Make copies of **Reproducible 1c: Journal Cover** and **Reproducible 1e: Reflections on a Star** for each child.

✓ *Tip*: Make extra reflection journal covers to have for children who are not here this week.

✓ *Tip*: Provide paper clips so that the children may secure their pages inside their journals until the last week when they staple their books together.

Older Children

- **Say:** Today you are going to begin making a reflection journal. You will add to your reflection journal every week during Advent. First you will make a cover for your journal.

- Invite each child to choose a piece of large construction paper.

- Have each child fold the construction paper in half by bringing the short sides together.

- Give each child a copy of **Journal Cover**.

- Encourage each child to use colored pencils, crayons, or markers to decorate the journal cover and add their name.

- Have each child cut out the cover and glue it onto the front of the construction paper folder.

- **Say:** Now you are ready to make the first page for your reflection journal.

- **Ask:** What Christmas story did we hear today? (the wise men following the star) How many times have you heard this story before?

- **Say:** Every year around Christmas we tell the same stories, don't we? These stories are familiar to us. It might be tempting to assume we know the stories and don't need to hear them again.

- **Ask:** Why do you think it's important to retell the stories of Jesus' birth every year? (Possible answers include: So we remember them. We might learn something new from them. They are important.)

- **Say:** Just as the star led the wise men to Jesus, the stories of Christmas point us to God. They remind us how much God loves us, and they remind us why we celebrate the birth of Jesus every year.

- Give each child a copy of **Reflections on a Star** and have the child write his or her name on it.

- Invite each child to spend time reading, reflecting, and writing.

- Have children place their papers inside their reflection journal covers.

- Collect the reflection journals to be used next week.

- Have the children sit in a circle.

- Invite the children to make the signs for wonder and star learned earlier in the lesson.

- **Pray:** God of wonder, thank you for the star that led the wise men to your Son, Jesus. Help us to pay attention this Advent season and look for ways we can share your love with others. Amen.

Magi Follow a Star
Based on Matthew 2:1-12

Magi #1: We are magi.

Magi #2: Some people call us wise men.

Magi #3: Some people call us wise guys!

Magi #1: We live east of Jerusalem. One day we saw a new star in the sky.

Magi #2: We wondered what it meant.

Magi #3: We did. That star made us wonder!

Magi #1: We thought the star might mean an important king was about to be born.

Magi #2: We decided to follow the star and find the king so we could honor him.

Magi #3: And the star led us to Bethlehem!

Magi #1: Well, not right away. We stopped in Jerusalem first and asked where we could find the child who has been born king of the Jews.

Magi #2: King Herod called together the chief priests and scribes and asked them where the king was to be born.

Magi #1: They told us a long time ago a prophet had said that the child would be born in Bethlehem.

Magi #3: So we went to Bethlehem!

Magi #1: King Herod encouraged us to continue searching and to let him know when we found the child.

Magi #2: Herod said he wanted to worship him also, but I'm not sure he was telling the truth.

Magi #1: We left King Herod and continued to follow the star.

Magi #2: We were very happy when the star stopped.

Magi #3: It stopped in Bethlehem!

Magi #1: The star stopped over a house. We were filled with joy!

Magi #2: When we went in the house we found the child, Jesus, with his mother, Mary, and we knew we had found the new king we were searching for.

Magi #3: We found him in Bethlehem!

Magi #1: We immediately knelt down and worshiped him.

Magi #2: We offered him gifts of gold, frankincense, and myrrh to honor him.

Magi #3: And we thanked God for leading us by a star all the way to Bethlehem!

Magi #1: When it was time to leave we remembered King Herod wanted us to come back and tell him where to find the child.

Magi #2: But we were warned in a dream not to go back to Herod.

Magi #3: So when we left Bethlehem, we went home a different way.

Triangle Stars

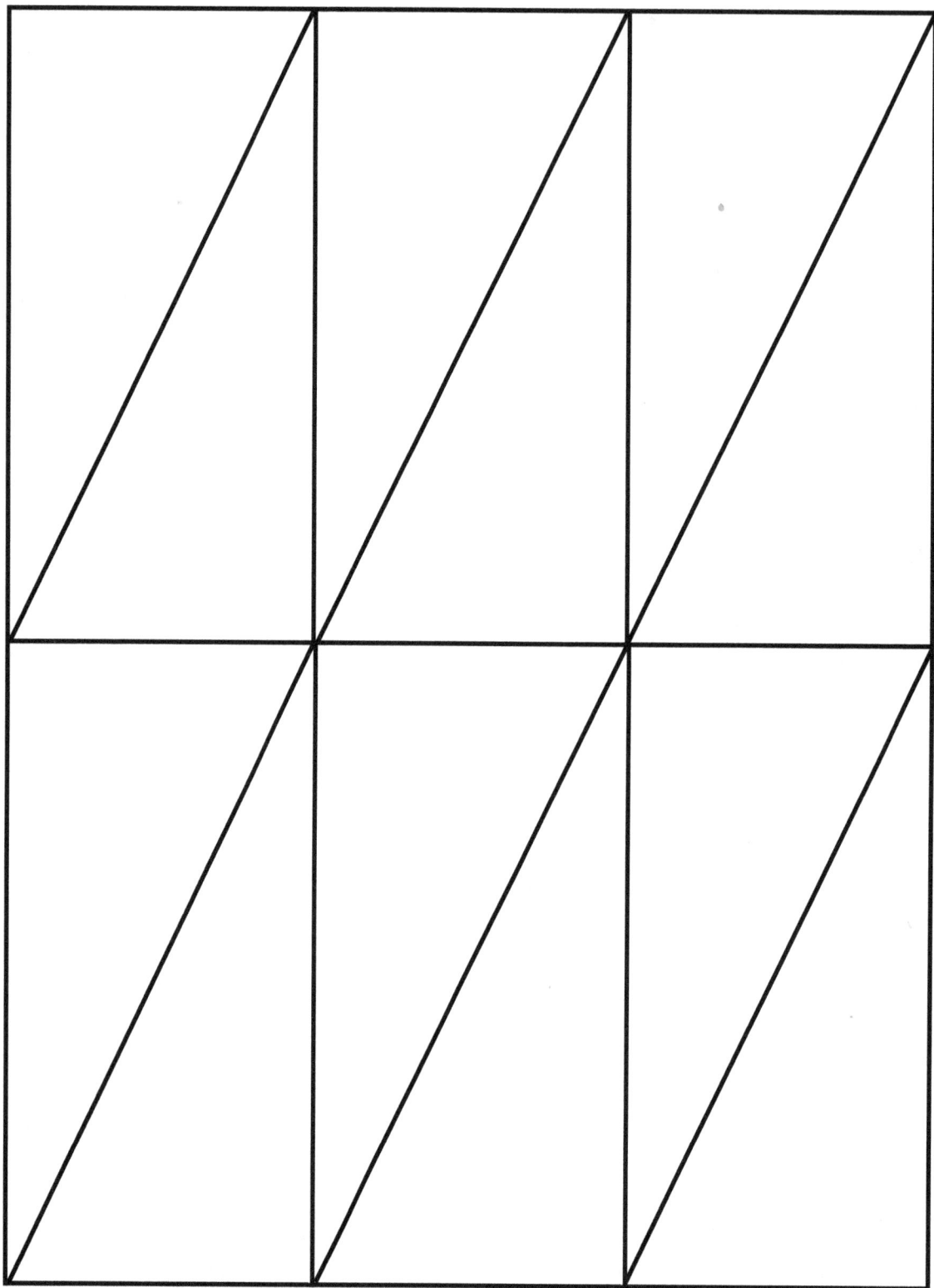

Journal Cover

My
Wonder of
Christmas
Journal

by _____

The Wonder of a Star

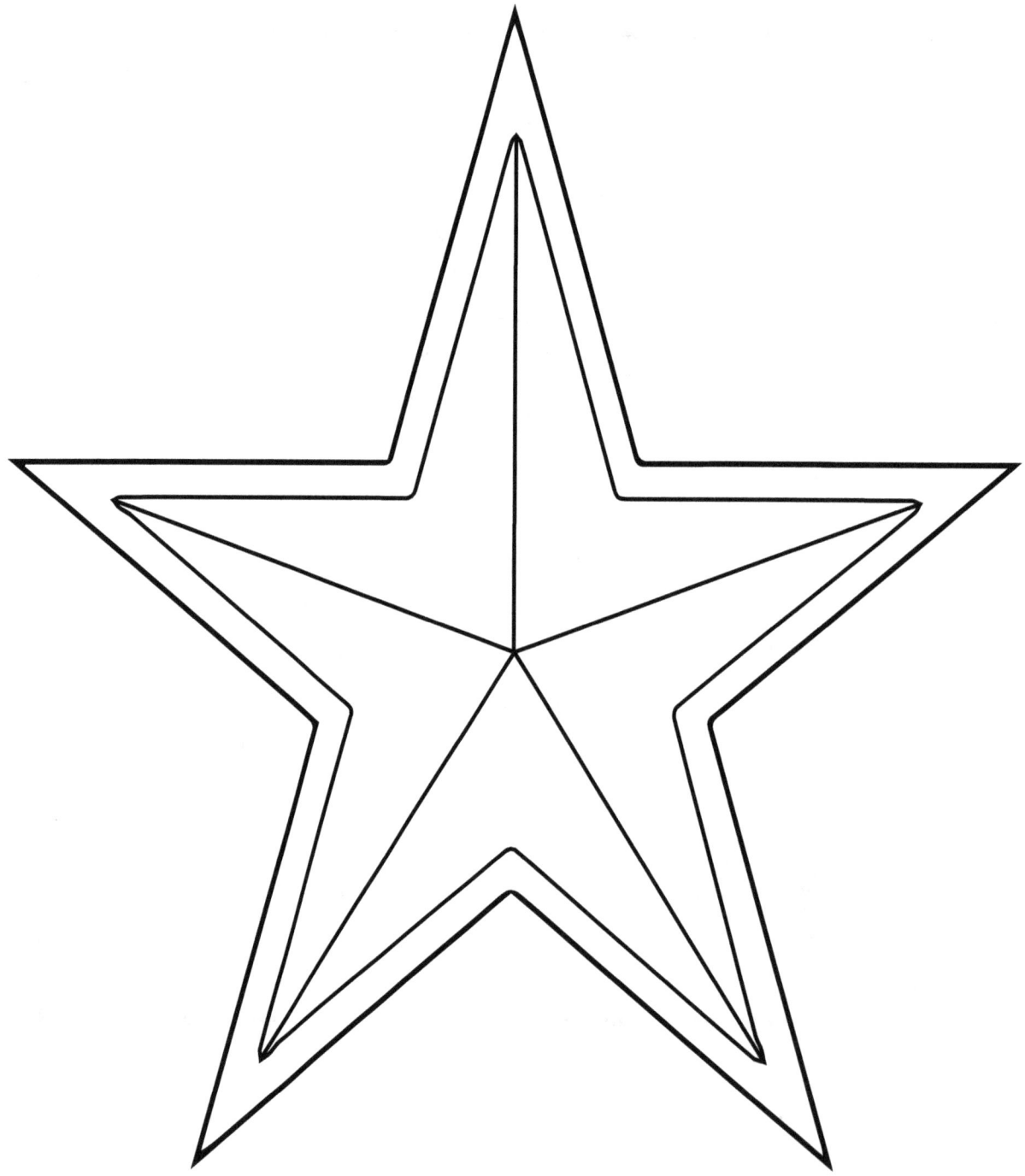

Reflections on a Star

The magi, or wise men, saw a new star and wondered what it meant. What are some things you wonder about?

_____

_____

_____

The wise men followed the star, and it led them to God's Son, Jesus. Who or what helps you connect with God?

_____

_____

_____

The magi brought gifts of gold, frankincense, and myrrh to honor Jesus as king. What are the ways you honor Jesus?

_____

_____

_____

If the wise men hadn't been paying attention, they would have missed the appearance of the new star. If the wise men hadn't followed the star, they would have missed meeting Jesus. What are the ways you see God at work in the world today when you pay attention?

_____

_____

_____

2 The Wonder of a Name

Focus for the Teacher

Of the four Gospels, only Matthew and Luke provide us with information about the birth of Jesus, and their accounts differ. Both Matthew and Luke tell of an angel messenger delivering the news that Jesus is to be born. However, Luke tells us of the angel's visit to Mary. In Matthew, the story of the angel's visit concerns Joseph.

Mary was a young girl, probably around fourteen—the age at which girls were married during Bible times. Mary was just an ordinary girl living in a small town, Nazareth in Galilee —until the angel's visit.

Overall, the Bible mentions very little about Joseph. We are told Joseph is a righteous man; this statement is supported by the fact that upon learning Mary was pregnant before they were married, Joseph made plans to divorce her quietly. In those days, once a couple was engaged, they were considered to be married. For Mary to become pregnant before they had marital relations would have been considered adultery. Mosaic Law required capital punishment under such cases. Joseph had already decided not to follow the law and have

> Jesus' name was chosen as a reminder that Jesus is our Savior.

Mary stoned to death, even before the angel appeared to him. After the angel's visit, Joseph took Mary as his wife. Doing so must have caused Joseph to be subject to more than a few questions. Joseph's willingness to trust God gives us a good idea of the type of man who was Jesus' earthly father.

Mary and Joseph were visited separately by the angelic messenger. However, the angel told both Mary and Joseph the baby was to be named Jesus. The name Jesus is the Greek version of the Hebrew name Joshua, meaning salvation. The angel offers an explanation for the name to Joseph, saying, "You will call him Jesus, because he will save his people from their sins" (Matthew 1:21).

As we continue our study of the wonders of Christmas, this week we explore the wonder of a name. The name given to Jesus was not an accident. Jesus' name was chosen as a reminder that Jesus is our Savior. God sent Jesus to remind us of God's never-ending love for us and to show us how God wants us to live.

Explore Interest Groups

Be sure adult leaders are waiting when the first child arrives. Greet and welcome the children. Get the children involved in an activity that interests them and introduces the theme for the day's activities.

Discover Today's Wonder Word

- **Say:** Today is the second week of *The Wonder of Christmas* study.
- **Ask:** Do you remember our wonder word from last week? (star)
- Show the children the poster you have prepared.
- **Say:** Today's wonder word is hidden on this poster. I wonder what today's word is.
- Invite the children to work together and use blue and purple markers to color over the entire poster. Because the marker will not cover the areas where the white crayon has been used, the hidden word will become visible. Show the children how to use the flat edge of the marker tip to color.
- **Ask:** What is today's wonder word? (name)
- **Say:** Today we will be discussing the wonder of a name!
- **Ask:** Since we are talking about the Christmas story, whose name do you think we will be talking about today? (Jesus)
- Display the finished poster in your classroom. Leave the poster on display throughout the study.

Prepare

- ✓ *Note*: Consider having all children participate in this activity since it provides the theme for today's lesson.
- ✓ Provide a large piece of posterboard, a white crayon, blue and purple markers, and tape.
- ✓ Use a white crayon to write the word name in large bubble letters on the posterboard.
- ✓ *Tip*: If the posterboard you are using has a shiny side, use the non-shiny surface of the posterboard for this activity.
- ✓ *Note*: If you have a large class, prepare multiple posters and divide the children into small groups for this activity.

Prepare

✓ Make copies of **Reproducible 2a: Jesus Ornament** on cardstock.

✓ Provide yarn, scissors, glue, and paper hole punches.

Name of Jesus Ornament

- **Say:** You are going to make an ornament of Jesus' name today.
- Give each child a copy of **Jesus Ornament**.
- Have the children cut out their ornaments along the solid line and use a paper punch to punch a hole at the top of the ornament where indicated by the circle.
- Invite each child to cut pieces of yarn and add them to the ornament to outline the word *Jesus*.
- Let each child continue to cut pieces of yarn and add them to the ornament to fill in the remaining space surrounding the letters.
- Encourage the children to add yarn to the backs of their ornaments also, if they like.
- **Say:** When you take your ornament home and hang it on your tree, it can remind you that Jesus is the name we celebrate.

Prepare

✓ Provide paper, magazines, scissors, and glue sticks.

✓ Look through the magazines and remove any pages that contain inappropriate pictures or articles.

Name Art

- **Say:** Our names are important. Today you are going to use your name to create art.
- Let children look through the magazines and cut out the letters in their own names. The letters may be any size, color, or style. Encourage children to cut out a lot of each letter.
- Give each child a piece of paper.
- Encourage each child to use the cut out letters to spell his or her name on the paper, gluing the letters in place.
- Have children keep working to spell their names until they have used all of the letters they cut, covering as much of the paper as possible.
- As the children are working, invite them to share stories of how their names were chosen. Encourage children who do not know the origin of their names to ask their family when they get home.

Deliver the Messages

- **Say**: Our names are important. Today you are going to use your Divide the children into teams.

- Have each team line up from one side of the room to the other.

- Have the children on each team turn sideways, hold their arms out to their sides, and spread themselves across the room so that there is about a foot of space between each pair of teammates' hands.

- **Say**: In today's Bible story we will hear about an angel delivering messages to Mary and Joseph. The messages the angel delivered to Mary and Joseph had something in common. The goal of this game is to deliver the message written on these index cards from one side of the room to the other. You may move your arms and hands, but you may not move your feet until all of your cards have been delivered to the other side of the room. Imagine your feet are stuck to the floor. Also, only one card may be passed down your line at a time. You'll have to communicate so you know where each card is and when the next card may be passed. When all of the cards have been delivered, the person collecting the cards will say, "Got it!" That is your cue to unstick your feet and help put the message in the right order.

- On one side of the room, place a set of index cards on the floor near the first child in each team's line.

- Once you've explained the game, encourage the children to play the game.

- **Ask**: What child was named Jesus? (Mary's baby, God's Son)

- **Say**: The angel told both Mary and Joseph what to name the baby.

Prepare

✓ Write the following message on index cards, one word per card: "The child will be named Jesus." You will need one set of cards for each team. Shuffle each set of cards.

✓ The number of children on each team will depend on the size of the area available to play the game. When the children line up, there should be enough space between them to make the game challenging.

Large Group

Bring all the children together to experience the Bible story. Use a bell to alert the children to the large group time.

Learn Some Signs

- **Say**: We are continuing to talk about wonder. Last week we learned how to say the word wonder using sign language. Let's review how to make the sign for wonder.

- Review the sign for wonder with the children: place your right index finger to your temple as if you are pointing to the side of your head, and move your finger in a small circle.

- Invite the children to make the sign for wonder with you.

- **Say**: Today we are talking about the wonder of a name.

- Teach the children the sign for name: Hold your hands in front of you with the index and middle fingers of each hand together as if pointing forward. Tap the two fingers of your right hand on top of the two fingers of your left hand two times.

- Invite the children to make the sign for name with you.

- **Ask**: Whose name do we celebrate at Christmas? (Jesus)

- Teach the children the sign for Jesus: Touch the middle finger of your right hand to the palm of your left hand. Then touch the middle finger of your left hand to the palm of your right hand.

- Invite the children to make the sign for Jesus with you.

- **Say**: Now let's sign the words wonder, name, and Jesus together.

- Encourage the children to sign the word wonder and then the word name and then the word Jesus.

Prepare

✓ Review the instructions for making the signs for *wonder*, *name*, and *Jesus* so you can teach them to the children.

The Wonder of Christmas: Children's Leader Guide

Control the Volume of the Bible Verse

- **Say:** Last week we learned a Bible verse that reminds us God created our wonderful world and loves us.

- Show the children the Bible verse as you say it aloud.

- **Say:** Now let's pretend I am a volume control slider—like on a computer screen or electronic device. We will say the verse together three times. When I am standing over here (move all the way to your right side) the volume needs to be very soft. As I walk across the room, the volume increases; and when I am standing over here (move all the way to your left side), the volume is very loud.

- Encourage the children to say the verse with you three times as you control the volume with your position.

- **Say:** Now let's sign the words wonder, name, and Jesus together.

- Encourage the children to sign the word wonder and then the word name and then the word Jesus.

Prepare

✓ Be sure the Bible verse you displayed last week is hanging where the children can see it. (Give thanks to the only one who makes great wonders—God's faithful love lasts forever. Psalm 136:4)

Name Him Jesus

- **Say:** Today is the second Sunday of Advent.
- **Ask:** What are we waiting and preparing for during Advent? (Christmas)
- **Say:** Last week we heard one of the stories of Christmas.
- **Ask:** What story did we hear last week? (the wise men following the star)
- **Say:** Last week we heard the story of the wise men following the star to find Jesus. And we learned that they found him after he was born and worshiped him. Today we are backing up and telling a story about some things that happened before Jesus was born.
- Read the Bible story from **Name Him Jesus**.
- **Say:** The angel told Mary and Joseph that the baby Mary was going to have was God's Son.
- **Ask:** How did Mary and Joseph know what to name the baby? (The angel told them to name the baby Jesus.)
- **Say:** The name *Jesus* means "salvation" or "one who saves." Jesus came to the world as a savior.

Prepare

✓ Provide copies of **Reproducible 2b: Name Him Jesus** for children to take home.

Prepare

✓ Provide a Nativity set and an Advent wreath with LED candles that will be used throughout the study.

✓ Set up a worship center by covering a table with a cloth. Add a Bible and the Advent wreath. Place the wise men figures from the Nativity set on one side of the table. If your Nativity set contains a stable, set the stable on the other side of the table. Place Mary and Joseph near the stable. Do not add the other pieces of the Nativity set to the worship center.

The Wonder of a Name

- **Say**: Today is the second Sunday of Advent and the second week of *The Wonder of Christmas* study.

- Invite a child to turn on one of the LED candles on the Advent wreath.

- **Say**: Last week we talked about the wonder of a star. The star led the wise men to Jesus. Celebrating Christmas leads us closer to God.

- Point out the wise men on the worship center.

- **Say**: Last week we heard how they followed the star and found Jesus after he was born, but this week we're backing up to an earlier part of the story. So our wise men are still traveling in search of Jesus.

- Invite a child to turn on a second LED candle on the Advent wreath.

- **Ask**: How many Sundays are there in Advent? (four)

- **Say**: Today we heard of the angel appearing to Mary and Joseph. I've added Mary and Joseph to our worship center.

- **Ask**: What does the name Jesus mean? (salvation or one who saves)

- **Say**: At the time Jesus was born, many people had strayed from following God's Word. People were not treating each other fairly or with kindness. God sent Jesus as a savior to remind people of God's love and to show people how God wanted them to live.

- **Ask**: Do we always remember how God wants us to live? Do we always treat people fairly and with kindness?

- **Say**: Jesus is our Savior. Jesus reminds us of God's love and teaches us how God wants us to live.

- **Pray**: God of wonder, thank you for your Son named Jesus. Thank you for sending Jesus to remind the world of your love for us and to show us how you want us to live. Amen.

- Dismiss children to their small groups.

Small Groups

Divide the children into small groups. You may organize the groups around age levels or around readers and nonreaders. Keep the groups small, with a maximum of ten children in each group. You may need to have more than one group of each age level.

Young Children

- **Say:** Last week you began making an art journal. Today you will add another page to your journal.

- Give the children their art journals.

- **Ask:** What was our wonder word last week? (star)

- **Say:** Last week we talked about the wonder of the star that led the wise men to Jesus.

- **Ask:** What is today's wonder word? (name)

- **Say:** Today we heard about the angel telling Mary and Joseph to name the baby Jesus. We are followers of Jesus, and Jesus is our Savior.

- **Ask:** What does it mean to be a follower of Jesus? (to follow Jesus' teachings, to live the way Jesus taught us to live)

- **Say:** We do our best to follow Jesus' teachings. Jesus taught us about God's love and about how God wants us to live. One of the things we do as Jesus' followers is to share God's love with other people.

- **Ask:** What are some ways you share God's love with others?

- Allow children an opportunity to share their ideas.

- **Say:** As we prepare to celebrate Christmas, we remember the gift of Jesus, our Savior. Sharing God's love is an excellent way to celebrate the wonder of Christmas.

- Give each child a copy of **The Wonder of a Name** and have the child write his or her name on it.

- Invite the children to decorate the name Jesus and draw a picture of a way they can share God's love with someone as they prepare to celebrate the birth of Jesus.

- Have children put their pages inside their art journal covers.

- Collect the art journals to be used next week.

- Have the children sit in a circle.

- Invite the children to make the signs for wonder, name, and Jesus learned earlier in the lesson.

- **Pray:** God of wonder, thank you for the gift of your Son, whose wonderful name, Jesus, reminds us of your love for us. Help us to share your love with others. Amen.

Prepare

- ✓ Make copies of **Reproducible 2c: The Wonder of a Name** for each child.

- ✓ Provide crayons and art journals started last week.

- ✓ Have extra art journals available for children who were not present last week.

- ✓ *Tip*: Provide paper clips so that the children may secure their pages inside their journals until the last week when they staple their books together.

Prepare

✓ Make copies of **Reproducible 2d: Reflections on a Name** for each child.

✓ Provide pencils and reflection journals started last week.

✓ Have extra reflection journals available for children who were not present last week.

✓ *Tip*: Provide paper clips so that the children may secure their pages inside their journals until the last week when they staple their books together.

Older Children

- **Say:** Last week you began making a reflection journal. Today you will add another page to your journal.

- Give the children their reflection journals.

- **Ask:** What was our wonder word last week? (star) What story of Christmas did we hear last week? (the story of the wise men following the star)

- **Say:** Let's work together to retell the Bible story we heard today.

- Have the children work together to retell the Bible story. Encourage children to share what they remember about the story. If necessary, ask questions to help children remember the story.

- **Say:** Good job working together to remember the story.

- **Ask:** What does it mean to be a follower of Jesus? How is your life different than it would be if you were not a follower of Jesus?

- Allow children an opportunity to share their thoughts and ideas.

- Give each child a copy of **Reflections on a Name** and have the child write his or her name on it.

- Invite each child to spend time reading, reflecting, and writing.

- Have children put their papers inside their reflection journals.

- Collect the reflection journals to be used next week.

- Have the children sit in a circle.

- Invite the children to make the signs for wonder, name, and Jesus learned earlier in the lesson.

- **Pray:** God of wonder, thank you for sending Jesus to be our Savior. As we prepare to remember and celebrate the birth of your Son, help us to share your love with others. Amen.

Jesus Ornament

J
E
S
U
S

Name Him Jesus
Based on Matthew 1:18-25 and Luke 1:26-33.

Hi! My name is Gabriel. You may not be able to tell by looking at me, but I'm an angel. Really, I am! One of my jobs as an angel is to deliver messages for God. I like doing that because I get to surprise people. Most people aren't expecting an angel to show up.

One time God sent me to Nazareth to deliver a message to a young girl named Mary. I said, "Hey, Mary! God loves you! I have a message for you from God."

At first, Mary was frightened by my appearance. I get that reaction a lot. Do I really look that scary? Don't answer that. I told Mary not to be afraid. Then I delivered God's message.

I told Mary she was going to have a baby. She told me I had made a mistake because she and her fiancé, Joseph, weren't married yet, but then I told her the baby was God's Son. "You will name him Jesus and he will do great things," I said. I reminded Mary that nothing is impossible for God.

Although I surprised Mary, she chose to trust God. She told me, "If this is God's plan for me, I'll do it."

That wasn't the only message I delivered about Mary's baby. I also delivered a message to Mary's fiancé, Joseph. When Mary told Joseph she was pregnant, he knew he wasn't the baby's father. According to the law, Joseph could have made a big deal out of this and embarrassed Mary in public and even had her killed. Because Joseph was a good man, he had decided to break off their engagement quietly.

This is where I came in. One night when Joseph was sleeping, God sent me to visit him in his dream. I delivered God's message. I said, "Joseph, son of David,"—you see, Joseph was a descendant of King David—"do not be afraid to take Mary as your wife. Her child is God's Son. When he is born, name him Jesus because he will save people."

I am proud to say I must have done a good job delivering God's message, because when Joseph woke up he did what God had told him and took Mary as his wife.

The Wonder of a Name

JESUS

Reflections on a Name

The angel told Mary and Joseph to name the baby Jesus. What does the name Jesus mean to you? How do you feel when you hear Jesus' name?

_____

_____

_____

_____

How does your family celebrate the birth of Jesus? Which family traditions help you celebrate Jesus?

_____

_____

_____

_____

God sent Jesus to the world as a reminder of God's never-ending love for us. How does it make you feel to know God loves you and will never stop loving you, no matter what?

_____

_____

_____

_____

3 The Wonder of a Manger

Objectives

The children will
• hear Luke 2:1-20.
• learn about Jesus' birth and the shepherds visiting Jesus.
• discover that Jesus is different than all other leaders and people.
• explore what it means to follow Jesus.

Theme

Jesus came to the world humbly, bringing peace.

Bible Verse

Give thanks to the only one who makes great wonders—God's faithful love lasts forever.

(Psalm 136:4)

Focus for the Teacher

"In those days Caesar Augustus declared that everyone throughout the empire should be enrolled in the tax lists" (Luke 2:1). At the time of Jesus' birth, Caesar Augustus was the most powerful person in the world, a world dominated by the Roman Empire. Therefore, when Emperor Augustus decided everyone needed to travel to his or her hometown to be registered, that was what happened. It didn't matter if that required a journey of eighty miles one way by foot or animal—long before that distance would be just over a one-hour trip in an automobile. And it didn't matter if the woman to whom you were engaged was about to have a baby. Emperor Augustus had decreed that the entire world would be registered so that everyone living in the Roman Empire could be made to pay taxes.

Joseph and Mary journeyed to Bethlehem, and when they arrived it was time for Mary's child to be born. Luke tells us there was no room for Joseph and Mary in the guestroom. Joseph and Mary were not the only ones who had traveled to Bethlehem to be registered. Therefore, Mary's baby was laid in an animal's feed trough on a

> God's Son began life humbly, with a manger for his bed.

bed of hay. God's Son began life humbly, having a manger for his bed. This was in stark contrast to the power of Emperor Augustus. It is highly unlikely Caesar was even aware of Jesus' birth.

Meanwhile, in a nearby field, shepherds were keeping watch over their sheep. It was these simple shepherds outside with their flocks who were the first to receive the news of Jesus' birth.

An angel visited them! The angel announced that a savior had been born in Bethlehem. In response to this surprising angelic announcement, the shepherds hurried off to Bethlehem, where they found the baby lying in a manger.

Once the shepherds had found Mary, Joseph, and the baby, they "returned home, glorifying and praising God for all they had heard and seen" (Luke 2:20). The shepherds discovered the wonder of the manger—that the birth of Jesus is reason for joy and celebration. Indeed, over two thousand years later the birth of that baby who was laid in a manger is still something to celebrate.

Explore Interest Groups

Be sure adult leaders are waiting when the first child arrives. Greet and welcome the children. Get the children involved in an activity that interests them and introduces the theme for the day's activities.

Discover Today's Wonder Word

- **Say**: Today is the third week of *The Wonder of Christmas* study.

- **Ask**: Do you remember our wonder words from the last two weeks? (star and name)

- Show the children the poster you have prepared.

- **Say**: Today's wonder word is hidden on this poster. I wonder what today's word is.

- Invite the children to work together and use blue and purple markers to color over the entire poster. Because the marker will not cover the areas where the white crayon has been used, the hidden word will become visible. Show the children how to use the flat edge of the marker tip to color.

- **Ask**: What is today's wonder word? (manger)

- **Say**: Today we will be discussing the wonder of a manger!

- **Ask**: Do you remember hearing about a manger in the Christmas story? (Jesus was laid in a manger when he was born.)

- Display the finished poster in your classroom. Leave the poster on display throughout the study.

Prepare

- ✓ *Note*: Consider having all children participate in this activity since it provides the theme for today's lesson.

- ✓ Provide a large piece of posterboard, a white crayon, blue and purple markers, and tape.

- ✓ Use a white crayon to write the word manger in large bubble letters on the posterboard.

- ✓ *Tip*: If the posterboard you are using has a shiny side, use the non-shiny surface of the posterboard for this activity.

- ✓ *Note*: If you have a large class, prepare multiple posters and divide the children into small groups for this activity.

Prepare

✓ Provide small clay pots (approximately 1 1/2-inch diameter), raffia, thin ribbon, wooden beads (1/2-inch), white felt, scrap paper, scissors, tacky glue, and black markers.

Make a Manger Ornament

- **Say:** Today you will make a manger ornament to remind you of Jesus' birth.

- Have each child cut a piece of ribbon approximately 12 inches long. Have them tie the ends of the ribbon together to form a ribbon loop.

- Give each child a clay pot. Have the children place a line of tacky glue on the inside of the pot, down one side, across the bottom and up the other side.

- Have the children lay their ribbon loop along the glue line with the end of the loop sticking out of the pot. Tell the children they will need to wait until the glue is completely dry before using the ribbon loop.

- Give the children some scrap paper, and have each child tear off small pieces of paper, crumpling them and placing them inside the pot until the pot is about 3/4 full.

- Have the children cut the raffia into small pieces about 1/2 inch to 2 inches long.

- Encourage each child to cover the top of the paper in the pot with glue.

- Let the children put their raffia pieces in the pot, pressing them down into the glue.

- Give each child a wooden bead.

- Have each child draw a face on the bead with a marker and glue the bead on top of the raffia at one side of the pot.

- Have each child cut a small piece of white felt (approximately 1 inch by 2 inches) and glue it on top of the raffia, next to the wooden bead, to represent the swaddling clothes that covered baby Jesus.

- **Say:** When you take your ornament home, let it remind you that Mary laid baby Jesus in a manger when he was born.

Make Edible Mangers

- **Say:** Today we are talking about the wonder of the manger. You are going to make a manger you can eat!

- Have the children wash their hands.

- Let the children place the butterscotch chips in the mixing bowl.

- Microwave the chips until melted. Be careful not to overcook the chips. Begin with 30 seconds and then microwave for 15-second intervals, having the children stir after each interval until the chips are melted and smooth. Note that the chips will retain their shape until stirred, even when melted.

- Have the children add the chow mein noodles to the melted butterscotch.

- Let the children stir the mixture until all of the noodles are coated.

- Give each child a piece of waxed paper and two pretzel twists.

- Place approximately 1/2 cup of noodle mixture on each child's waxed paper.

- Instruct the children to mold the noodles into a mound and place a pretzel on each end to resemble a manger.

- Give the children wet wipes to clean their hands.

- **Say:** We will let your mangers set up or harden, and you can take them with you when you go home today.

- At the end of the lesson, place each manger in a resealable plastic bag to send home.

Prepare

✓ Provide chow mein noodles (6 oz.), butterscotch chips (11 or 12 oz.), small pretzel twists, microwave-safe mixing bowl, spoon, microwave, waxed paper, quart-size resealable plastic bags, and wet wipes.

✓ *Note:* This recipe makes eight edible mangers. Make additional batches if you have more than eight children in your class.

Going to the Manger Game

- Have the children stand in a circle.

- **Say**: In today's Bible story we will hear how the shepherds heard about Jesus' birth and went to Bethlehem to see him.

- **Ask**: Do you remember where Mary laid Jesus after he was born? (in a manger)

- **Say**: Mary laid Jesus in a manger, and that's where the shepherds found him when they arrived in Bethlehem. We are going to play a game called "Going to the Manger."

- Explain the following rules to the children:
  o   One person will begin the game by describing how they are going to the manger—by running, walking, skipping, hopping, jumping, flying, etc. The person will say, "I'm going to the manger, and I'm going to (chosen action)."
  o   Then we will all do the action the person has named. If the person has said they will run, we will run in place for a few seconds. If the person says they will fly, we'll pretend to fly.
  o   The next person will say, "I'm going to the manger, and I'm going to (chosen action)."
  o   We all then will do the first action named, followed by the second action named.
  o   Each time a person tells us how they are going to the manger, we'll add that action on the list as we act out all of the actions.

- Encourage the children to play the game.

Large Group

Bring all the children together to experience the Bible story. Use a bell to alert the children to the large group time.

Learn Some Signs

- **Say:** We are continuing to talk about wonder. We have learned how to say the word *wonder* using sign language. Let's review how to make the sign for wonder.

- Review the sign for wonder with the children: Place your right index finger to your temple as if you are pointing to the side of your head, and move your finger in a small circle.

- Invite the children to make the sign for wonder with you.

- **Say:** Today we are talking about the wonder of a manger.

- Teach the children the sign for manger: Hold your hands in front of you with palms up. Move your hands away from each other and slightly upward as you turn the palms to face each other, as if you were making the sides of a manger.

- Invite the children to make the sign for manger with you.

- **Say:** Now let's sign the words *wonder* and *manger* together.

- Encourage the children to sign the word *wonder* and then sign the word *manger*.

Prepare

✓ Review the instructions for making the signs for *wonder* and *manger* so you can teach them to the children.

Prepare

✓ Provide copies of
**Reproducible 3a:
Jesus Is Born** for
children to take home.

Jesus Is Born

- **Say:** We are going to use our five senses to experience today's Bible story.

- **Ask:** What are the five senses? (sight, smell, hearing, taste, and touch)

- **Say:** I am going to read the Bible story. As I read, close your eyes and pretend you are in the story. Imagine what you would have seen, smelled, heard, tasted, and felt. After you've heard the story, we'll talk about what you experienced.

- Invite the children to close their eyes.

- Read the Bible story from **Jesus Is Born**.

- Invite the children to open their eyes.

- **Ask:** What did you imagine seeing as you heard the story?

- Allow the children to share their thoughts.

- Repeat the question for each of the remaining four senses, allowing the children time to respond to each question.

- **Say:** This is the story we remember and celebrate every year. The birth of Jesus is very good news!

The Wonder of a Manger

- **Say:** Today is the third Sunday of Advent.
- Invite a child to turn on one of the LED candles on the Advent wreath.
- **Say:** Two weeks ago we talked about the wonder of a star. The star led the wise men to Jesus. Celebrating Christmas leads us closer to God.
- Point out the wise men on the worship center.
- **Say:** Our wise men are still traveling in search of Jesus. It took them a long time to follow the star to Bethlehem!
- Invite a child to turn on a second LED candle on the Advent wreath.
- **Say:** Last week we heard about the angel telling Mary and Joseph to name the baby Jesus. We talked about the wonder of a name.
- **Ask:** Do you remember what the name Jesus means? (one who saves or savior)
- **Say:** Jesus is our Savior.
- Invite a child to turn on a third LED candle on the Advent wreath.
- **Ask:** How many Sundays are there in Advent? (four)
- **Say:** We are getting closer to Christmas! Today we heard the story of Jesus' birth and the shepherds' visit.
- **Ask:** Where did Mary lay Jesus after he was born? (a manger)
- **Say:** A manger seems like an unusual bed for the Son of God! Jesus is God's Son, but he didn't come into the world in a flashy, attention-getting way. His birth wasn't treated like the birth of an important king or celebrity. Instead, his birth was announced to shepherds out in the field.
- **Ask:** Why do you think God chose such a humble, unusual way to enter the world?
- Allow children to share their thoughts and ideas.
- **Say:** Jesus came into the world in a surprising and unexpected way. Jesus was different from the rulers and kings whom people at the time were used to. In fact, Jesus is different than the leaders and kings alive today. Jesus came to teach us about peace.
- **Pray:** God of peace and love, thank you for loving us. Thank you for sending your Son, Jesus, to teach us your way to live. Amen.
- Dismiss children to their small groups.

Prepare

✓ Provide a Nativity set and an Advent wreath with LED candles that will be used throughout the study.

✓ Set up a worship center by covering a table with a cloth. Add a Bible and the Advent wreath. Place the wise men figures from the Nativity set on one side of the table. Place the rest of the Nativity set on the other side of the worship center. Use all pieces of the Nativity set this week.

Prepare

✓ Be sure the Bible verse you displayed the first week is hanging where the children can see it. (Give thanks to the only one who makes great wonders— God's faithful love lasts forever. Psalm 136:4)

Bible Verse Round

- Show the children the Bible verse as you say it aloud.

- Encourage the children to read the verse with you.

- **Say:** God, who is the Creator of all wonders in the world, loves us! This verse reminds us of this.

- Divide the children into three groups. Assign each group a number: one, two, or three.

- **Say:** We are going to say the verse two more times. This time we will say it as a round. That means each group will start and stop at different times. The second group will start after the first group says, "one." The third group will start after the second group says, "one." You will need to pay attention to the others in your group so you can stay together.

- Encourage the children to say the verse twice as a round, cueing each group when to come in.

The Wonder of Christmas: Children's Leader Guide

Small Groups

Divide the children into small groups. You may organize the groups around age levels or around readers and nonreaders. Keep the groups small, with a maximum of ten children in each group. You may need to have more than one group of each age level.

Young Children

- **Say:** You have been making an art journal. It is time to add another page to your journal.
- Give the children their art journals.
- **Say:** So far we have talked about the wonder of a star and the wonder of a name.
- **Ask:** Who followed the star to find Jesus? (the wise men) What name did we talk about? (Jesus)
- **Say:** Today we heard about Mary laying Jesus in a manger after he was born. That's an interesting choice for a baby bed. Jesus came into the world in a humble way. When Jesus grew up, he taught people about choosing to live peacefully and love each other.
- **Ask:** What does it mean to live in peace? (to love each other, to choose not to fight)
- **Say:** As followers of Jesus, it's our job to look for ways to spread peace in God's world.
- **Ask:** What are some ways you can choose peace in your life? How could you teach others about peace?
- Allow children an opportunity to share their thoughts and ideas.
- Give each child a copy of **The Wonder of a Manger** and have the child write his or her name on it.
- Invite each child to draw a Nativity picture.
- Allow children time to draw.
- Affirm each child's work.
- Have children put their pages inside their art journal covers.
- Collect the art journals to be used next week.
- Have the children sit in a circle.
- Invite the children to make the signs for wonder and manger learned earlier in the lesson.
- **Pray:** God of wonder, thank you for the gift of your Son, Jesus, whose first bed was a manger. Help us to follow Jesus' teachings of peace and to share your love with others. Amen.

Prepare

- ✓ Make copies of **Reproducible 3b: The Wonder of a Manger** for each child.
- ✓ Provide crayons and art journals started two weeks ago.
- ✓ Have extra art journals available for children who were not present the last two weeks.
- ✓ *Tip:* Provide paper clips so that the children may secure their pages inside their journals until the last week when they staple their books together.

Prepare

✓ Make copies of **Reproducible 3c: Reflections on a Manger** for each child.

✓ Provide pencils and reflection journals.

✓ Have extra reflection journals available for children who were not present the last two weeks.

✓ *Tip*: Provide paper clips so that the children may secure their pages inside their journals until the last week when they staple their books together.

Older Children

- **Say:** It is time to add another page to your reflection journal.

- Give the children their reflection journals.

- **Ask:** What was our wonder word two weeks ago? (star) What story of Christmas did we hear that week? (the story of the wise men following the star)

- **Say:** The star led the wise men to Jesus. Celebrating Christmas leads us closer to God.

- **Ask:** What was our wonder word last week? (name)

- **Say:** The name of Jesus means Savior. Jesus is our Savior.

- Give each child a copy of **Reflections on a Manger** and have the child write his or her name on it.

- **Say:** Today we heard the story of Jesus' birth. When Jesus was born, Mary laid him in a manger.

- **Ask:** Do you know what a manger is usually used for?

- **Say:** A manger is a feeding trough for animals. Not a usual bed for a baby!

- Invite each child to spend time reading, reflecting, and writing.

- Have children put their papers inside their reflection journals.

- Collect the reflection journals to be used next week.

- Have the children sit in a circle.

- Invite the children to make the signs for wonder and manger learned earlier in the lesson.

- **Pray:** God of wonder, thank you for sending Jesus to be a different kind of leader. Help us to follow the teachings of Jesus and share your love with others. Amen.

Jesus Is Born
Based on Luke 2:1-20

In those days Caesar Augustus declared that everyone throughout the empire should be enrolled in the tax lists. This first enrollment occurred when Quirinius governed Syria. Everyone went to their own cities to be enrolled. Since Joseph belonged to David's house and family line, he went up from the city of Nazareth in Galilee to David's city, called Bethlehem, in Judea. He went to be enrolled together with Mary, who was promised to him in marriage and who was pregnant. While they were there, the time came for Mary to have her baby. She gave birth to her firstborn child, a son, wrapped him snugly, and laid him in a manger, because there was no place for them in the guestroom.

Nearby shepherds were living in the fields, guarding their sheep at night. The Lord's angel stood before them, the Lord's glory shone around them, and they were terrified.

The angel said, "Don't be afraid! Look! I bring good news to you—wonderful, joyous news for all people. Your savior is born today in David's city. He is Christ the Lord. This is a sign for you: you will find a newborn baby wrapped snugly and lying in a manger." Suddenly a great assembly of the heavenly forces was with the angel praising God. They said, "Glory to God in heaven, and on earth peace among those whom he favors."

When the angels returned to heaven, the shepherds said to each other, "Let's go right now to Bethlehem and see what's happened. Let's confirm what the Lord has revealed to us." They went quickly and found Mary and Joseph, and the baby lying in the manger. When they saw this, they reported what they had been told about this child. Everyone who heard it was amazed at what the shepherds told them. Mary committed these things to memory and considered them carefully. The shepherds returned home, glorifying and praising God for all they had heard and seen. Everything happened just as they had been told.

The Wonder of a Manger

Reflections on a Manger

Jesus is a king, but he came to the world in a humble, unexpected way. What might you expect the birth of a king to be like? How might a king's birth be announced?

_____

_____

_____

How is Jesus a different kind of king?

_____

_____

_____

As a follower of Jesus—who teaches us a way of peace and love—how is your life different than if you did not follow Jesus?

_____

_____

_____

What do you think the world would be like if everyone treated each other with love and lived together peaceably?

_____

_____

_____

What are some ways you can work for peace in God's world?

_____

_____

_____

4 The Wonder of a Promise

Objectives

The children will
- hear Isaiah 7:14 and 9:6-7.
- learn about Isaiah's prophecy of Jesus' birth.
- discover that Jesus symbolizes God's promise to be with us.
- explore what it means to experience God's presence in their lives.

Theme

Jesus is Immanuel—God with us.

Bible Verse

Give thanks to the only one who makes great wonders—God's faithful love lasts forever.

(Psalm 136:4)

Focus for the Teacher

Many years before Jesus' birth, the prophet Isaiah told of God's promise to send a savior. In Isaiah 7:14 we hear the promise, "The young woman is pregnant and is about to give birth to a son, and she will name him Immanuel." Immanuel means "God is with us." The birth of Jesus fulfilled a promise God had made.

Isaiah's message of a promised Messiah was delivered to people who were in need of just such a message of hope. Isaiah lived about five hundred years after God had delivered the Israelites from slavery in Egypt. Many of the Israelite people had failed to put their trust in God and had begun worshiping other gods. The people were looking to alliances with other countries to protect them instead of putting their trust in God. This was a time of social injustice, exploitation of the poor, and corruption of political and religious leaders. Does this sound familiar? Many of the issues facing the Israelites are ones we continue to struggle with today.

Isaiah warned the people of Israel that they needed to repent of their wrongdoing and put their trust, once again, in God. Amidst the

> The birth of Jesus fulfilled a promise God had made.

warnings, in the ninth chapter of Isaiah we find a message of hope: God would send a savior. In Isaiah 9:6, the attributes of the promised savior are described. The coming Messiah would be the ideal king, representing the best qualities of Israel's past kings. He would be a wise leader (Wonderful Counselor). He would be powerful (Mighty God). He would display fatherly love and care (Everlasting Father). He would bring peace and prosperity (Prince of Peace). Isaiah's description of the promised leader and peaceful times ahead brought hope to a weary world.

Though it may seem unusual to end this Advent study with the words of Isaiah spoken over seven hundred years before Jesus was born, Isaiah's words remind us of an important part of the Christmas story: the wonder of a promise. Our world is much different than when Isaiah lived, yet we still long for the peace Isaiah foretold. We still need to be reminded of God's promise—the promise made long ago and fulfilled by Jesus. The birth of Jesus, our Immanuel, means we are never alone—God is with us.

Explore Interest Groups

Be sure adult leaders are waiting when the first child arrives. Greet and welcome the children. Get the children involved in an activity that interests them and introduces the theme for the day's activities.

Discover Today's Wonder Word

- **Say**: Today is the last week of *The Wonder of Christmas* study.

- **Ask**: Do you remember our previous wonder words? (star, name, and manger)

- Show the children the poster you have prepared.

- **Say**: Today's wonder word is hidden on this poster. I wonder what today's word is.

- Invite the children to work together and use blue and purple markers to color over the entire poster. Because the marker will not cover the areas where the white crayon has been used, the hidden word will become visible. Show the children how to use the flat edge of the marker tip to color.

- **Ask**: What is today's wonder word? (promise)

- **Say**: Today we will be discussing the wonder of a promise! The birth of Jesus was the fulfillment of a promise God made many years before Jesus was born.

- Display the finished poster in your classroom.

Prepare

- ✓ *Note*: Consider having all children participate in this activity since it provides the theme for today's lesson.

- ✓ Provide a large piece of poster board, a white crayon, blue and purple markers, and tape.

- ✓ Use a white crayon to write the word promise in large bubble letters on the posterboard.

- ✓ *Tip*: If the posterboard you are using has a shiny side, use the non-shiny surface of the posterboard for this activity.

- ✓ *Note*: If you have a large class, prepare multiple posters and divide the children into small groups for this activity.

Names for Jesus

- Give each child a copy of **Names for Jesus** and a pencil.

- Encourage each child to solve the puzzle.

- **Ask**: Which of these names for Jesus have you heard before? Are any of the names of Jesus new to you? What do these names tell you about the kind of leader Jesus was?

- **Answers**: Wonderful Counselor, Mighty God, Eternal Father, Prince of Peace

Prepare

- ✓ Make copies of **Reproducible 4a: Names for Jesus**.

- ✓ Provide pencils.

Prepare

✓ Make copies of **Reproducible 4b: Scroll Ornament** for each child.

✓ Provide straws, tape, glue, string, scissors, colored pencils, crayons, and markers.

✓ Cut the straws into pieces approximately 3 inches long.

Make a Scroll Ornament

- **Say:** Two weeks ago we heard about an angel telling Mary and Joseph what to name God's Son when he was born.

- **Ask:** What was the baby to be named? (Jesus)

- **Say:** Jesus is called by many names. We talked about Jesus meaning Savior. Today in our Bible story we will hear some other names for Jesus. One of those names is Immanuel. You are going to make a scroll ornament with the name Immanuel on it.

- Give each child a copy of **Scroll Ornament** and a pair of scissors.

- Have each child cut the ornament out along the solid lines.

- Give each child two pieces of straw.

- Encourage each child to use a small piece of tape to tape the top edge of the ornament to one piece of straw, taping along the length of the straw. Have each child use another small piece of tape to tape the bottom edge of the ornament to the other piece of straw.

- Have each child roll the top straw forward toward the writing on the ornament until the straw piece is covered by the paper. Secure the paper in place with a small amount of glue. Repeat this process with the bottom straw. The ornament should now resemble a scroll, with the word *Immanuel* visible between each end of the scroll.

- Let each child cut a piece of string approximately 10 inches long.

- Have each child thread the string through the top straw and tie the ends together to form a hanging loop.

- Encourage each child to use colored pencils, crayons, or markers to decorate the ornament.

Wonder Review

- Have the children sit down.

- **Say:** For the last few weeks we have been hearing the stories of Christmas. We are going to play a game to review the stories. I will read some statements. If the statement is true, jump to your feet and shout, "Ding, ding, ding!" If the statement is not true, remain seated and say, "Buzz!"

- Read the following statements to the children, encouraging them to respond appropriately.
  o The wise men saw a new star in the sky and wondered what it meant. (Ding, ding, ding!)
  o The wise men decided the new star meant it was time to order pizza. (Buzz!)
  o The wise men followed the star to Bethlehem. (Ding, ding, ding!)
  o The wise men brought gifts of gold, frankfurters, and mistletoe to honor Jesus. (Buzz!)
  o The wise men went and told King Herod where to find Jesus. (Buzz!)
  o An angel told Mary she was going to have a baby. (Ding, ding, ding!)
  o The angel told Mary the baby was God's Son. (Ding, ding, ding!)
  o The angel told Mary to name the baby Jedidiah. (Buzz!)
  o When Joseph found out Mary was going to have a baby, he planned to divorce her quietly. (Ding, ding, ding!)
  o An aardvark appeared to Joseph in a dream and told him Mary's baby was God's Son. (Buzz!)
  o The angel told Joseph to name the baby Harold. (Buzz!)
  o Joseph and Mary traveled to Bethlehem to register for the tax lists. (Ding, ding, ding!)
  o While Joseph and Mary were in Bethlehem, Jesus was born. (Ding, ding, ding!)
  o When Jesus was born, Mary laid him in a fancy crib. (Buzz!)
  o The first people to hear the news of Jesus' birth were the shepherds. (Ding, ding, ding!)
  o The shepherds read about Jesus' birth in the newspaper. (Buzz!)
  o After the angel told them about Jesus' birth, the shepherds hurried to Bethlehem to find him. (Ding, ding, ding!)
  o The shepherds found Joseph, Mary, and Jesus at the shopping mall. (Buzz!)
  o After the shepherds saw Jesus, they told everyone they saw the good news of Jesus' birth. (Ding, ding, ding!)

- **Say:** Great job! You know the stories of Christmas.

Large Group

Bring all the children together to experience the Bible story. Use a bell to alert the children to the large group time.

Prepare

✓ Review the instructions for making the signs for *wonder* and *promise* so you can teach them to the children.

Learn Some Signs

- **Say:** This is our last week talking about the wonder of Christmas. We have learned how to say the word *wonder* using sign language. Let's review how to make the sign for wonder.

- Review the sign for wonder with the children: Place your right index finger to your temple as if you are pointing to the side of your head and move your finger in a small circle.

- Invite the children to make the sign for wonder with you.

- **Say:** Today we are talking about the wonder of a promise.

- Teach the children the sign for promise: Place your right index finger in front of your lips. Bring your right hand down and place your flat right hand on top of your left fist.

- Invite the children to make the sign for promise with you.

- **Say:** Now let's sign the words *wonder* and *promise* together.

- Encourage the children to sign the word *wonder* and then sign the word *promise*.

Prepare

✓ Provide copies of **Reproducible 4c: Isaiah's Prophecy and God's Promise** for children to take home.

Isaiah's Prophecy and God's Promise

- **Say:** Today is the last Sunday of Advent.

- **Ask:** What have we been waiting and preparing for during Advent? (Christmas, Jesus' birth)

- **Say:** We have been hearing the stories of Christmas, which is about Jesus' birth. Our Bible story today is about something that happened seven hundred years before Jesus was born. It is about a prophet named Isaiah.

- Read the story from **Isaiah's Prophecy and God's Promise**.

- **Ask:** How long is Advent? (Four weeks)

- **Say:** Imagine if you had to wait seven hundred years for Christmas instead of four weeks!

- **Ask:** How do you think the people felt when they were waiting such a long time for the promised savior to be born? (Discouraged, tired of waiting, impatient)

- **Say:** Even though they had to wait a long time, the people kept waiting and hoping because they knew God had promised a savior and they knew God would keep that promise.

The Wonder of a Promise

- **Say:** Today is the fourth and last Sunday of Advent.
- Invite a child to turn on one of the LED candles on the Advent wreath.
- **Say:** Three weeks ago we talked about the wonder of a star. The star led the wise men to Jesus. Celebrating Christmas leads us closer to God.
- Point out the wise men on the worship center.
- **Say:** Our wise men are still traveling in search of Jesus. They are almost to Jesus.
- Invite a child to turn on a second LED candle on the Advent wreath.
- **Say:** Two weeks ago we heard about the angel telling Mary and Joseph to name the baby Jesus. We talked about the wonder of a name.
- **Ask:** Do you remember what the name Jesus means? (one who saves or Savior)
- **Say:** Jesus is our Savior.
- Invite a child to turn on a third LED candle on the Advent wreath.
- **Say:** Last week we heard the story of Jesus' birth and the shepherds' visit.
- **Ask:** Where did Mary lay Jesus after he was born? (a manger)
- **Say:** Jesus came to the world in an unexpected way. His birth was announced to shepherds out in the field. Jesus is different from other kings and leaders.
- Invite a child to turn on the fourth LED candle on the Advent wreath.
- **Say:** All of our candles are lit now. It is almost Christmas!
- **Ask:** What was God's promise that Isaiah told the people about? (God would send a Savior, a new leader)
- **Say:** Isaiah said God promised to send a new leader for the people. Isaiah said the child who would be born to lead the people would be named Immanuel.
- **Ask:** Do you remember what Immanuel means? (God with us.)
- **Say:** Jesus is God's Son. One of Jesus' names is Immanuel. Jesus was God's Son sent to earth. The birth of Jesus was the fulfillment of God's promise that Isaiah told the people about.
- **Pray:** Loving God, thank you for the gift of love you gave us by sending your Son, Jesus.
- Dismiss children to their small groups.

Prepare

- ✓ Provide a Nativity set and an Advent wreath with LED candles.
- ✓ Set up a worship center by covering a table with a cloth. Add a Bible and the Advent wreath. Place the Nativity set on the worship center. Place the wise men near to the rest of the Nativity pieces, but not quite with them.

Prepare

✓ Be sure the Bible verse you displayed the first week is hanging where the children can see it. (Give thanks to the only one who makes great wonders— God's faithful love lasts forever. Psalm 136:4)

Creative Voice Bible Verse

- Show the children the Bible verse as you read it aloud.
- **Ask**: Who is the one who makes great wonders? (God the Creator)
- How long will God love us? (forever)
- Encourage the children to read the verse with you.
- Invite a child to choose a type of voice to use to say the Bible verse (loud, soft, squeaky, slow, bouncy, fast, and so forth).
- Encourage the class to say the Bible verse in the type of voice chosen by the child.
- Invite a new child to choose a voice.
- Say the Bible verse several times in this manner.

Small Groups

Divide the children into small groups. You may organize the groups around age levels or around readers and nonreaders. Keep the groups small, with a maximum of ten children in each group. You may need to have more than one group of each age level.

Young Children

- **Say:** Today you will finish the art journal you have been making.

- Give the children their art journals.

- **Say:** So far we have talked about the wonder of a star, the wonder of a name, and the wonder of a manger.

- **Ask:** Who followed the star to find Jesus? (the wise men) What name did we talk about? (Jesus) Who used a manger for a bed? (Jesus)

- **Say:** Today we heard about Isaiah's prophecy about Jesus' birth. Many years before Jesus was born, Isaiah told people God promised to send a new leader. Isaiah said the new leader's name would be Immanuel. Jesus is Immanuel.

- **Ask**: Do you remember what Immanuel means? (God with us.)

- Give each child a copy of **The Wonder of a Promise** and have the child write his or her name on it.

- **Say**: Jesus' birth kept God's promise. God is always with us. No matter what. That's a promise you can trust.

- **Ask:** How does it make you feel to know God is always with you?

- Allow children an opportunity to share their thoughts.

- Invite each child to draw a picture of his or her family remembering and celebrating the birth of Jesus.

- Allow children time to draw.

- Affirm each child's work.

- Have children put their pages inside their art journal covers.

- Staple each child's art journal along the folded edge, making sure to staple through all pages.

- **Say:** Today you may take your art journals home with you.

- Have the children sit in a circle.

- Invite the children to make the signs for wonder and promise learned earlier in the lesson.

- **Pray:** God of wonder, thank you for promising to send Immanuel and for sending your Son, Jesus. Help us to share your love with others as we celebrate the birth of Jesus. Amen.

Prepare

- ✓ Make copies of **Reproducible 4d: The Wonder of a Promise** for each child.

- ✓ Provide crayons, staplers, and art journals.

- ✓ Have extra art journals available for children who are present for the first time this week.

Prepare

✓ Make copies of **Reproducible 4e: Reflections on a Promise** for each child.

✓ Provide pencils, staplers, and reflection journals.

✓ Have extra reflection journals available for children who are present for the first time this week.

Older Children

- **Say:** Today you will finish your reflection journal.

- Give the children their reflection journals.

- **Ask:** What was our wonder word the first week of Advent? (star) What story of Christmas did we hear that week? (the story of the wise men following the star)

- **Say:** The star led the wise men to Jesus. Celebrating Christmas leads us closer to God.

- **Ask:** What was our wonder word the second week of Advent? (name)

- **Say:** The name of Jesus means Savior. Jesus is our Savior.

- **Ask:** What was our wonder word last week? (manger)

- **Say:** A manger was a surprising first bed for God's son.

- Give each child a copy of **Reflections on a Promise** and have the child write his or her name on it.

- **Say:** Today we heard the story of Isaiah telling people about God's promise to send Immanuel.

- **Ask:** How many years after Isaiah's prophecy was Jesus born? (over seven hundred years)

- Invite each child to spend time reading, reflecting, and writing.

- Have children put their papers inside their reflection journals.

- Staple each child's reflection journal along the folded edge, making sure to staple through all pages.

- **Say:** Today you may take your reflection journals home with you.

- Have the children sit in a circle.

- Invite the children to make the signs for wonder and promise learned earlier in the lesson.

- **Pray:** God of wonder, thank you for keeping your promise to send Immanuel. As we remember and celebrate Jesus' birth, help us look for ways to share your love with others. Amen.

Names for Jesus

Many years before Jesus was born, the prophet Isaiah spoke of a child who would be born and grow into a great leader. Use the key below to decode the following words and discover what Isaiah said this leader would be called.

__ __ __ __ __ __ __ __ __   __ __ __ __ __ __ __ __ __
23 15 14 4 5 18 6 21 12   3 15 21 14 19 5 12 15 18

__ __ __ __ __ __   __ __ __
13 9 7 8 20 25   7 15 4

__ __ __ __ __ __ __   __ __ __ __ __ __
5 20 5 18 14 1 12   6 1 20 8 5 18

__ __ __ __ __ __   __ __   __ __ __ __ __
16 18 9 14 3 5   15 6   16 5 1 3 5

Key:
A-1 B-2 C-3 D-4 E-5 F-6 G-7 H-8 I-9 J-10 K-11 L-12 M-13 N-14
O-15 P-16 Q-17 R-18 S-19 T-20 U-21 V-22 W-23 X-24 Y-25 Z-26

Scroll Ornament

Immanuel

Isaiah's Prophecy and God's Promise

Based on Isaiah 7:14, 9:6-7

Many years ago there lived a prophet named Isaiah. A prophet is a person who speaks for God. Isaiah delivered many messages from God during his lifetime.

At the time Isaiah was alive, God's people were not very happy. People were not always treated fairly. Some people were forgetting to trust God and were worshiping other gods. One of the messages Isaiah delivered from God was a message of hope. Isaiah told of a person who would come to lead God's people and be their savior. He said a baby would be born and be named Immanuel, which means God is with us. This baby would be a descendent of Jesse, who was King David's father.

Isaiah told the people what this savior would be like. He would be a leader who would have authority. Isaiah said this leader would be called Wonderful Counselor, Mighty God, Eternal Father, and Prince of Peace. These names describe a leader who is wise, understanding, strong, caring, and a builder of peace.

Over seven hundred years after Isaiah told God's people about God's promise to send a savior, Jesus was born. That's a long time to wait! Even though it took a long time, God's promise was kept. God sent Jesus, who was born as a baby, just as the prophet Isaiah had foretold. One of the names Jesus is called is Immanuel. Jesus' birth showed that God will always be with us.

The Wonder of a Promise

Jesus is Immanuel—God with us.

Draw a picture of your family remembering
and celebrating Jesus' birth.

Reflections on a Promise

The birth of Jesus fulfilled God's promise to send a new leader and savior. Say a silent prayer right now thanking God for keeping God's promise.

Jesus is Immanuel—God with us. The birth of Jesus was God's way of telling us we never have to be alone. How does it make you feel to know God is always with you?

_____

_____

_____

What does it mean to you to know God is with you when you are happy, joyful, and celebrating?

_____

_____

_____

How does it make you feel to know God is with you when you are sad, lonely, or confused?

_____

_____

_____

When we share God's love with others, we remind them of God's promise to always be with them. Who can you share God's love with as a way to remember and celebrate Jesus' birth?

_____

_____

_____